LEGAL NOTICE

WORDS FROM THE AUTHOR

As a Doctor of Neuroscience, my research on the biological mechanisms of learning has contributed to advancing science. Ironically, all this knowledge proved quite useless when faced with a 4-year-old child refusing to go to bed, rolling on the floor for no apparent reason, or choosing the word "no" as her personal motto.

This is how the idea for this trilogy came to me, aiming to promote the learning of children through 7 key rules at home, outside the home, or regarding hygiene. To achieve this, I drew inspiration from the work of the American psychologist Lawrence Kohlberg on moral development to create the different characters embodying authority. Indeed, from ages 3 to 8, a child adapts their behavior to avoid punishments. It is through this prism that the child defines what is "Good or No Good."

Furthermore, an often-neglected aspect of learning is oral expression during decision-making. When reading with your child, I recommend letting them verbalize their choices (along with hand gestures) when indicating who is behaving "Good" and who is behaving "No Good".

Beyond the learning aspect, my foremost hope is that the dialogues and illustrations will captivate your child's interest.

The illustrated children's book of choices

Good

or

No Good

THE TRILOGY

7 rules at home
7 rules outside the house
7 rules of hygiene

VALENTIN LANGLAIS

The illustrated children's book of choices

Good

or

No Good

7 rules at home

VALENTIN LANGLAIS

GRANT, the Elephant Judge :
Hey you there who's looking at me!
Hello.
What's your name?

I'm Grant the Elephant Judge. Being a judge is a job where we reward people who do something Good and punish those who do something No Good.

I have several animals to judge based on 7 rules to follow at home, and I need your opinion to make my decisions.

Could you please help me? Let me know which of the two following animals is behaving well and which is not behaving well. Also, don't hesitate to tell me why you think it's Good or No Good.

Do you understand what you need to do? You have an elephant's memory, indeed! Let's get started!

RICKEY, the Donkey:

My rider is asking me to go for a ride with him.

No, no, and no! Come on, fall off, you goof!

ORSON, the Horse:

My rider asks me to move slowly.
Alright, I'll walk at a gentle pace.

GRANT, the Elephant Judge:

My verdict is:
ORSON, the Horse *behaves* **Good!**
RICKEY, the Donkey *behaves* **No Good!**

Obeying
is Good!

Disobeying
is No Good!

AMANDA, the Panda:

*I don't want to do my lessons or learn.
It's much better to play all the time!*

EAGAN, the Eagle:

Don't disturb me, please.
I will play after my chores are done.

GRANT, the Elephant Judge:
My verdict is:
EAGAN, the Eagle *behaves* **Good!**
AMANDA, the Panda *behaves* **No Good!**

Doing your homework
is Good!

Only wanting to play
is No Good!

BETHEL, the Beetle:
It feels good to come home.
Hop!
I take off one shoe after the other.

BRIGGS, the Pig:

It was so much fun jumping in the rain and mud with my boots! What? Why are you looking at me?

GRANT, the Elephant Judge:

My verdict is:

BETHEL, the Beetle behaves **Good!**

BRIGGS, the Pig behaves **No Good!**

Removing your shoes when entering
is Good!

Keeping your shoes on
is No Good!

LOLA, the Koala:

Sorry! I made a mistake.
I'm the one who broke my sister's toy.
I'm really sorry.

MAXIMUS, the Hippopotamus:

No, it wasn't me who ate all the yellow fruits!

I promise!

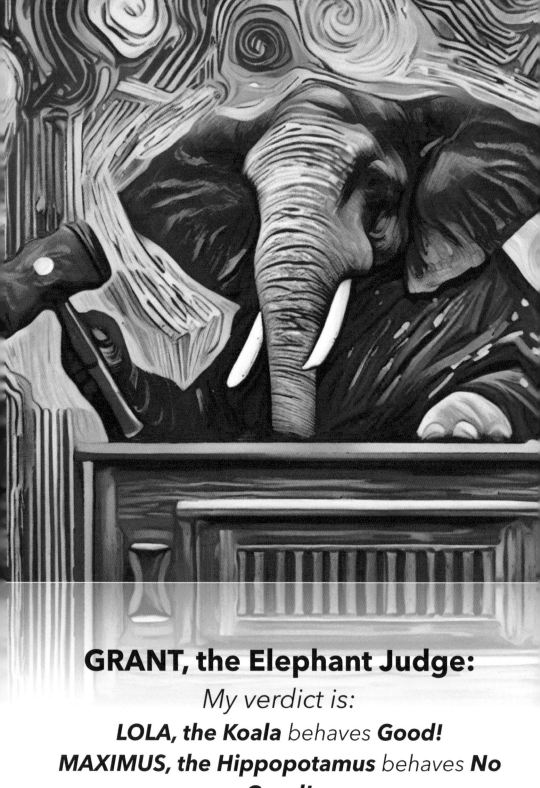

GRANT, the Elephant Judge:

My verdict is:
LOLA, the Koala *behaves* **Good!**
MAXIMUS, the Hippopotamus *behaves* **No Good!**

Telling the Truth
is Good!

Lying
is No Good!

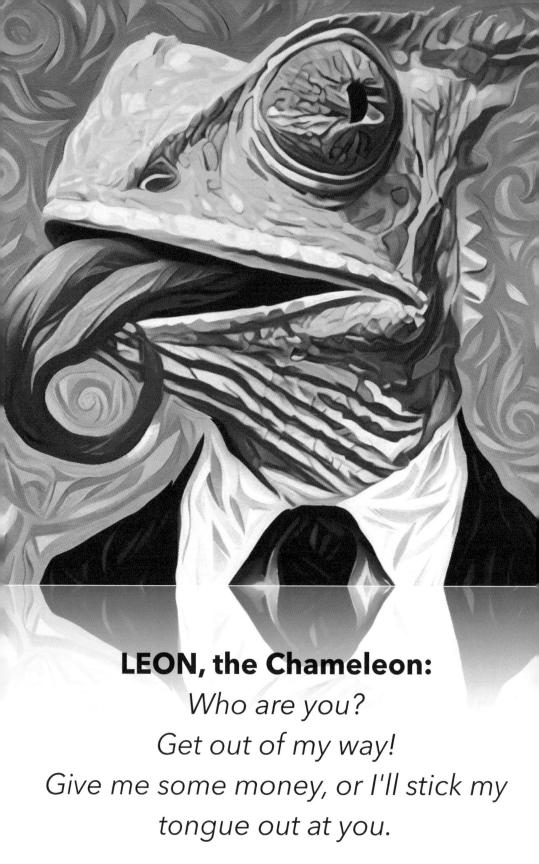

LEON, the Chameleon:
Who are you?
Get out of my way!
Give me some money, or I'll stick my tongue out at you.

ROSS, the Rhinoceros:
Hello.
Thank you very much for coming to see me. Please excuse me, but I have to leave. See you soon.

GRANT, the Elephant Judge:

My verdict is:
ROSS, the Rhinoceros *behaves* **Good!**
LEON, the Chameleon *behaves* **No Good!**

Being polite
is Good!

Being rude
is No Good!

MARGO, the Flamingo:
If you stay calm,
it's easy to balance on one leg.
And all that, in silence.

CYRUS, the Taurus:

I want someone to play with me!
DAD! MOM!
I'm going to sulk
if no one plays with me!

GRANT, the Elephant Judge:
My verdict is:
MARGO, the Flamingo *behaves* **Good!**
CYRUS, the Taurus *behaves* **No Good!**

Behaving wisely
is Good!

Making whims
is No Good!

GIGI, the Giraffe:
Yuck, vegetables!
I won't eat them.
I prefer candy!

KATE, the Cat:

I'm not a big fan of broccoli and carrots.

But I'll at least try to eat a few.

GRANT, the Elephant Judge:
My verdict is:
KATE, the Cat *behaves* **Good!**
GIGI, the Giraffe *behaves* **No Good!**

Eating vegetables is Good!

Eating nothing but sweets is No Good!

GRANT, the Elephant Judge:
*It's good. We're done.
You've been a great help.
A thousand thanks!*

Let's recap the rules we've established together.

At home, you need to:

1. **Obey**

2. **Do your homework**

3. **Take off your shoes when entering**

4. **Tell the truth**

5. **Be polite**

6. **Behaving wisely**

7. **Eat vegetables**

Now that you know perfectly what is **Good**

or No Good, I count on you to apply these rules in your daily life.

Thanks again, and I look forward to working together again!

The illustrated children's book of choices

Good

 or

No Good

7 rules outside the house

VALENTIN LANGLAIS

MAXIMILIAN, the Magician Judge:
Well, here's a nice surprise!
Welcome.
What's your name?

I am Maximilian the Magician Judge.

Being a judge is a job where we reward people who do something Good and punish those who do something No Good.

I have more than one trick up my sleeve, but at my age, a little help wouldn't hurt. I have several magical beings to judge based on 7 rules to follow outside the house, and I need your opinion to make my decisions.

Let me know which of the two following animals is behaving well and which is not behaving well. Also, don't hesitate to tell me why you think it's Good or No Good. Is everything clear for you?

Perfect! Let's begin!

BRYANT, the Giant :
Oops!
Hehe, I just farted on you!
Poopyhead!

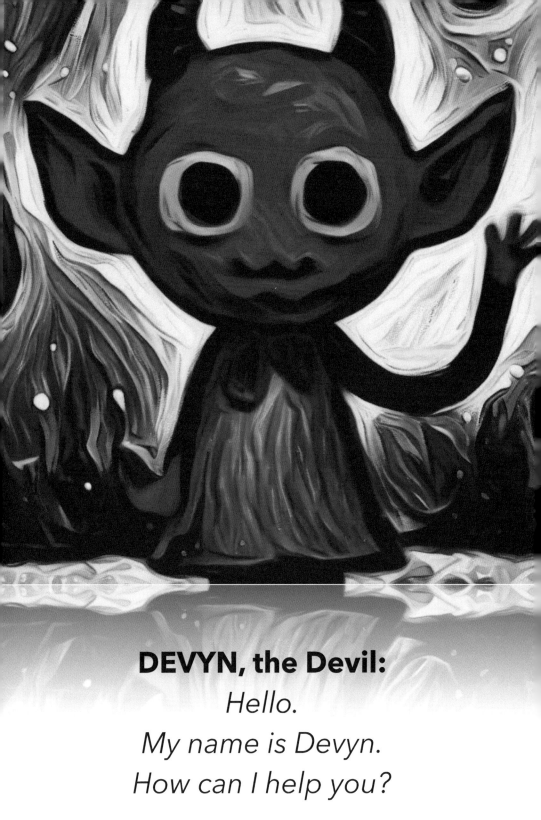

DEVYN, the Devil:
Hello.
My name is Devyn.
How can I help you?

MAXIMILIAN, the Magician Judge:

I've made my decision:
DEVYN, the Devil *behaves* **Good!**
BRYANT, the Giant *behaves* **No Good!**

Being courteous
is Good!

Being gross
is No Good!

ELLIE, the Elf:

*If you want to play with my toys,
no problem,
I'll lend them to you.*

GAVIN, the Goblin:
Gold is mine!
I love GOLD!
Especially when it's not mine!
Gold, gold, gold!

MAXIMILIAN, the Magician Judge:

I've made my decision:
ELLIE, the Elf *behaves* **Good!**
GAVIN, the Goblin *behaves* **No Good!**

Sharing
is Good!

Stealing
is No Good!

ROBIN, the Robot:
I am big and powerful!
I am...
THE SUPREME DESTROYER!
ATTACK!

AIRI, the Fairy:

*If you're not feeling well,
then let me comfort you
and help you.*

MAXIMILIAN, the Magician Judge:

I've made my decision:
AIRI, the Fairy *behaves* **Good!**
ROBIN, the Robot *behaves* **No Good!**

Protecting others is Good!

Hurting others is No Good!

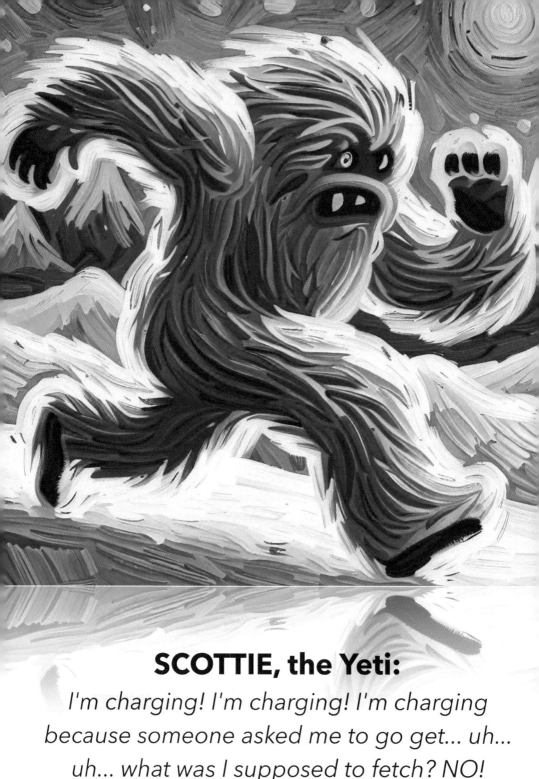

SCOTTIE, the Yeti:

*I'm charging! I'm charging! I'm charging
because someone asked me to go get... uh...
uh... what was I supposed to fetch? NO!
I left before hearing the end!
Quick, I'm charging again!*

MARCUS-JULIUS-ATTICUS, the Cerberus:

I patiently await my master's return for him to give me his orders. Like Head #1, I patiently wait for my master's return to receive his commands. I also, like Head #2, do as Head #1 does and patiently await my master's return for him to give me his orders.

MAXIMILIAN, the Magician Judge:

I've made my decision:
MARCUS-JULIUS-ATTICUS, the Cerberus
behaves **Good!**
SCOTTIE the Yeti *behaves* **No Good!**

Being Patient
is Good!

Being Impatient
is No Good!

DWAYNE, the Dwarf:

At school, I often have trouble understanding things at first. But by staying focused and persisting a bit, I always manage to succeed.

MADISON, the Dragon:

At school, I am the smartest. While my classmates keep thinking, I get bored.
So, why not...
BREATHE FIRE WHILE WAITING?!

MAXIMILIAN, the Magician Judge:

I've made my decision:
DWAYNE, the Dwarf *behaves* **Good!**
MADISON, the Dragon *behaves* **No Good!**

Staying focused at school
is Good!

Being inattentive at school
is No Good!

BJORN, the Unicorn:

The road is dangerous for children. Stay by my side, take my paw, and let's cross it together.

CRISTIAN, the Martian:
Looking before crossing the road is for babies!
A car behind me?
OH! CRASH!

MAXIMILIAN, the Magician Judge:

I've made my decision:
BJORN, the Unicorn *behaves* **Good!**
CRISTIAN, the Martian *behaves* **No Good!**

Holding hands across the road
is Good!

Crossing the road carelessly
is No Good!

ANGELINE, the Angel:

When I see someone alone, I go talk to them so they don't feel isolated anymore. And who knows, maybe we'll become friends.

CASSANDRA, the Hydra:
You're BAD!
You're UGLY!
That's why you don't have any friends.
HAHAHAHA!

MAXIMILIAN, the Magician Judge:
I've made my decision:
ANGELINE, the Angel *behaves* **Good!**
CASSANDRA, the Hydra *behaves* **No Good!**

Being Kind
is Good!

Being Mean
is No Good!

MAXIMILIAN, the Magician Judge:
And there you go, it's finished.
It's magical how time flies when you work well.

Let's recap the rules we've established together.

Outside the house, you need to:

1. **Be polite**

2. **Share**

3. **Protect others**

4. **Be patient**

5. **Be focused at school**

6. **Hold hands when crossing the road**

7. **Be kind**

Now that you know perfectly what is **Good or No Good**, I count on you to apply these rules in your daily life.

Thank you very much for your help.

See you soon, partner!

Good

or

No Good

7 rules of hygiene

VALENTIN LANGLAIS

VICTOR, the Alligator Judge:
Well, a new face.
You're adorable.
What's your name?

I am Victor the Alligator Judge.

Being a judge is a job where we reward people who do something Good and punish those who do something No Good.

I have several animals to judge based on 7 rules of hygiene, and I need your opinion to make my decisions.

I have a lot of teeth but not a lot of time, so you're going to help me. Let me know which of the two following animals is behaving well and which is not behaving well. Also, don't hesitate to tell me why you think it's Good or No Good.

Start without me. I'll join you after you've made your first choice.

DEVON, the Lion:

After eating, I use a toothbrush with gazelle-flavored toothpaste. The king of the jungle must have beautiful teeth.

SETH, the Marmoset:
In the evening, after eating a banana, I go straight to bed.
Look at my beautiful smile!

VICTOR, the Alligator Judge:

Upon reflection:
DEVON, the Lion *behaves* **Good!**
SETH, the Marmoset *behaves* **No Good!**

Brushing your teeth
is Good!

Not brushing your teeth
is No Good!

LILITH, the Rabbit:
Some soap.
A bit of water.
I rub. And I rinse.
Mmm! My hands smell good!

SWAYZEE, the Chimpanzee:
I come back from the bathroom and I'm going straight to dinner. YUCK! Why does my food taste like poop?

VICTOR, the Alligator Judge:
Upon reflection:
LILITH, the Rabbit *behaves* **Good!**
SWAYZEE, the Chimpanzee *behaves* **No Good!**

Washing your hands is Good!

Having dirty hands is No Good!

SKYLER, the Skunk:
I don't understand why people avoid me.
After all, I have a beautiful suit.

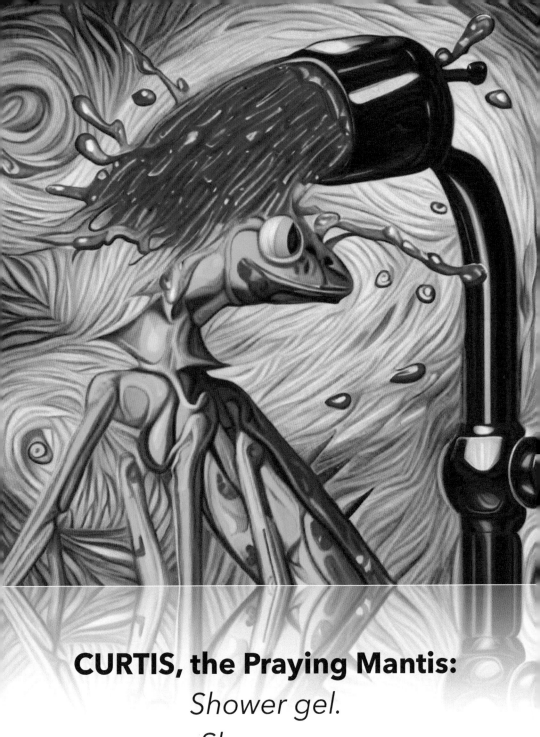

CURTIS, the Praying Mantis:
Shower gel.
Shampoo.
OH LA LA!
I smell good!

VICTOR, the Alligator Judge:

Upon reflection:

CURTIS, the Praying Mantis *behaves* **Good!**
SKYLER, the Skunk *behaves* **No Good!**

Washing your body
is Good!

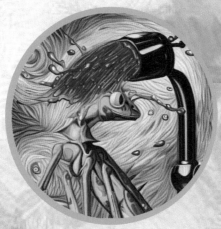

Not showering
is No Good!

TURNER, the Turtle:
I'm sitting comfortably.
Ah, I'm done.
Feeling better.

ESTER, the Hamster:

No! I don't want to go to the bathroom!
Oh NO!
I peed my pants!

VICTOR, the Alligator Judge:

Upon reflection:

TURNER, the Turtle *behaves* **Good!**

ESTER, the Hamster *behaves* **No Good!**

Going to the bathroom is Good!

Not going to the bathroom is No Good!

SLOANE, the Sloth:

After a busy day, there's nothing better than a good night's sleep.

BRYSON, the Bison:
DAD!!!
DAD!!!
I can't sleep!

VICTOR, the Alligator Judge:
Upon reflection:
SLOANE, the Sloth *behaves* **Good!**
BRYSON, the Bison *behaves* **No Good!**

Sleeping
is Good!

Getting up at
is No Good!

STEVEN, the Raven:

CROAK!

I don't want to go out.

CROAK!

I want to stay at home.

DAMIAN, the Dalmatian:
WOOF!
Nothing better than fresh air and going for a walk in the park.
WOOF!

VICTOR, the Alligator Judge:

Upon reflection:
DAMIAN, the Dalmatian *behaves* **Good!**
STEVEN, the Raven *behaves* **No Good!**

Getting fresh air outside
is Good!

Always staying inside
is No Good!

TESS, the Tigress:
More vegetables? No!
I wanted to eat meat. I'm not happy,
so I'm not going to eat or drink lunch.

ELLIOT, the Parrot:
Delicious! Delicious! Delicious! You know what? Food with a bit of water is... DELICIOUS!

VICTOR, the Alligator Judge:

Upon reflection:
ELLIOT, the Parrot *behaves* **Good!**
TESS, the Tigress *behaves* **No Good!**

Eating and Drinking Well
is Good!

Refusing to eat or drink

is No Good!

VICTOR, the Alligator Judge:

All these judgments have opened my appetite...
Ah ah, just kidding!
Thank you very much for your help!

Let's recap the rules we've established together.

For good hygiene, you need to:

1. **Brush your teeth**

2. **Wash your hands**

3. **Wash your body**

4. **Go to the toilet**

5. **Sleep**

6. **Get some fresh air outside**

7. **Eat well and stay hydrated**

Now that you know perfectly what is **Good or No Good**, I count on you to apply these rules in your daily life.

Farewell, delightful human!

THE TRILOGY
Good or No Good
Available on Amazon

valentin.langlais.author@gmail.com